THE
SUN, STARS,
AND GALAXIES

the solar system

THE
SUN, STARS,
AND GALAXIES

Edited by Michael Anderson

Britannica®
Educational Publishing
IN ASSOCIATION WITH

ROSEN
EDUCATIONAL SERVICES

Published in 2012 by Britannica Educational Publishing
(a trademark of Encyclopædia Britannica, Inc.)
in association with Rosen Educational Services, LLC
29 East 21st Street, New York, NY 10010.

Distributed exclusively by Rosen Educational Services.
For a listing of additional Britannica Educational Publishing titles, call toll free (800) 237-9932.

First Edition

Britannica Educational Publishing
Michael I. Levy: Executive Editor, Encyclopædia Britannica
J.E. Luebering: Director, Core Reference Group, Encyclopædia Britannica
Adam Augustyn: Assistant Manager, Encyclopædia Britannica

Anthony L. Green: Editor, Compton's by Britannica
Michael Anderson: Senior Editor, Compton's by Britannica
Sherman Hollar: Associate Editor, Compton's by Britannica

Marilyn L. Barton: Senior Coordinator, Production Control
Steven Bosco: Director, Editorial Technologies
Lisa S. Braucher: Senior Producer and Data Editor
Yvette Charboneau: Senior Copy Editor
Kathy Nakamura: Manager, Media Acquisition

Rosen Educational Services
Jeanne Nagle: Senior Editor
Nelson Sá: Art Director
Cindy Reiman: Photography Manager
Matthew Cauli: Designer, Cover Design
Introduction by Jeanne Nagle

Library of Congress Cataloging-in-Publication Data

The sun, stars, and galaxies / edited by Michael Anderson.—1st ed.
  p. cm.—(The solar system)
"In association with Britannica Educational Publishing, Rosen Educational Services."
Includes bibliographical references and index.
ISBN 978-1-61530-519-3 (library binding)
1. Sun—Juvenile literature. 2. Stars—Juvenile literature. 3. Galaxies—Juvenile literature. I.
Anderson, Michael.
QB521.5.S87 2012
523—dc22

                                                                            2011002628

Cover, back cover Shutterstock.com; pp. 10, 22, 35, 43, 59, 68, 76, 86, 88, 90, 93, 94 © www.istockphoto.
com/Brandon Alms; pp.21, 30, 31, 42, 45, 46, 65, 66, 74, 79 © www.istockphoto.com/Sergii Tsololo;
remaining interior background image © www.istockphoto.com/ Amanda Rohde

CONTENTS

*T*winkle, twinkle, little star
    How I wonder what you are

Readers of this book will wonder no more. In these pages lies information on the properties and characteristics of stars, including one star that is vital to life on Earth, the Sun. Topics include star composition, brightness, and configuration into constellations; the layers of the Sun and its role as the center of the solar system; and the shape of and energy emitted by large groups of stars known as galaxies. The scientific exploration of these illuminated celestial bodies through the years is also covered.

Up above the world so high
Like a diamond in the sky

The common image of stars as tiny points of light softly twinkling in the night sky belies their truly awesome power. Even their births are intense. Stars are formed when gravity forces a cloud of dust and debris to contract, causing a violent collision of hydrogen atoms. This high level of intensity carries through the life of a star as its core, or nucleus, burns courtesy of continuous explosions that are like nuclear bombs detonating. Eventually all the "fuel" in the core gets used up, and many stars simply collapse in upon themselves. This process leaves a small core that will eventually burn itself out as it cools. Some stars, however, go out in spectacular fashion as supernovas, exploding into vast fields of debris that eventually contribute to the creation of new stars.

In the vast scheme of the universe, the Sun is a pretty average star. It is estimated to be nearly 5 billion years old, which means it still has billions of years to shine before it reaches the end of its life cycle. Size-wise, the Sun falls somewhere in the middle between massive giants and tiny dwarfs. Within the solar system, however, the Sun is anything but average. Here, it is the center of all the action. A full 99 percent of the solar system's mass is taken up by the Sun. (Eight planets and their satellites, the dwarf planets, and an assortment of meteors, asteroids, and other celestial bodies account for the remaining 1 percent.) Although it is roughly the same size as billions of other stars, the Sun appears larger because it is relatively close (93 million miles/150 million kilometers) to Earth.

At the center of the Sun is the core, an extremely dense, pressure-filled collection

Stephan's Quintet, a group of galaxies with stars of many ages and colors, as seen from the Hubble Space Telescope. NASA, ESA, and the Hubble SM4 ERO Team

of atomic particles. Heat and light are emitted from the photosphere, which is the Sun's surface layer. The photosphere is in constant motion due to rolling solar waves. Another characteristic of the photosphere is sunspots, which are cooler dark patches caused by strong magnetic activity. Higher levels of the Sun's atmosphere are the chromosphere and the corona, which are not as visible as the photosphere but are actually much hotter.

Planets orbit the Sun, but the Sun has an orbit of its own, around the center of the Milky Way galaxy. The Milky Way is just one of many of these enormous collections of stars that make up the universe. A galaxy consists of millions or even hundreds of billions of stars in any of a variety of shapes: elliptical, spiral, barred spiral, or irregular (which seem kind of formless). The Milky Way is a spiral galaxy.

Twinkle, twinkle, little star
Now I know just what you are

THE SUN: THE CENTER OF THE SOLAR SYSTEM

Although the Sun is a rather ordinary star, it is very important to the inhabitants of Earth. The Sun is the source of virtually all Earth's energy.

approximate size of Earth

A huge cloud of gas erupts from the Sun. (The image is in false color and was taken in extreme ultraviolet light.) An image of Earth has been superimposed to show how enormous the Sun is in comparison. **SOHO/ESA/NASA**

It provides the heat and light that make life on Earth possible. Yet Earth receives only about half a billionth of the energy that leaves the Sun.

The Sun is a huge ball of hot gases. Like other stars, it produces enormous amounts of energy by converting hydrogen to helium deep within its interior.

POSITION IN SPACE

The Sun lies at the center of the solar system. It contains more than 99 percent of the system's mass. The immense pull of its gravity holds the planets, dwarf planets, asteroids, comets, and other bodies in orbit around it. The average distance between the Sun and Earth is roughly 93 million miles (150 million kilometers).

Light travels through space at about 186,282 miles (299,792 kilometers) per second, so a ray of sunlight takes only about 8 minutes to reach Earth. Light from other stars takes much longer to reach Earth; light from the next nearest star, Proxima Centauri, takes more than four years to arrive. The Sun is in the outer part of the Milky Way galaxy. Light from the center of the galaxy takes many thousands of years to reach Earth.

An illustration of the solar system, with the Sun at its center.
Shutterstock.com

Because the Sun is so close to Earth, it seems much larger and brighter than other stars. It is the only star whose surface details can be observed from Earth.

BASIC PROPERTIES

Stars vary greatly in size and color. They range from giant stars, which are much larger than the Sun, to dwarf stars, which can be much smaller than the Sun. In color they range from whitish blue stars with very high surface temperatures (more than 30,000 Kelvin, or 53,500° F) to relatively cool red stars (less than 3,500 K, or 5,840° F). (The Kelvin temperature scale uses degrees of the same size as Celsius, or centigrade, degrees, but it is numbered from absolute zero, -273.15° C.) The Sun is a yellow dwarf star, a kind that is common in the Milky Way galaxy. It has a surface temperature of about 5,800 K (10,000° F). Its diameter is about 864,950 miles (1,392,000 kilometers), which is about 109 times the diameter of Earth. Its volume is about 1,300,000 times Earth's volume, and its mass, or quantity of matter, is some 333,000 times as great as Earth's mass.

More than 90 percent of the Sun's atoms are hydrogen. Most of the rest are helium, with much smaller amounts of heavier elements such as carbon, nitrogen, oxygen, magnesium, silicon, and iron. By mass, the Sun is about 71 percent hydrogen and 28 percent helium.

The Sun has no fixed surface. It is much too hot for matter to exist there as a solid or liquid. Rather, the Sun's matter consists of gas and plasma, a state in which gases are heated so much that the electrons are stripped away from their atomic nuclei. The heated gas is said to be ionized because it consists of a group of ions, or electrically charged particles. The free electrons carry a negative charge, and the atomic nuclei carry a positive charge.

Like the planets, the Sun rotates. Because the Sun is not solid, different parts of it rotate at different rates. The parts of the surface near the equator spin the fastest, completing one rotation about every 25 Earth days. The parts of the surface near the poles take 36 days to complete a rotation.

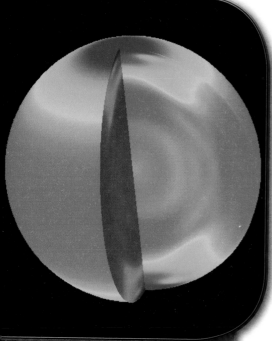

A false-color Doppler image shows rotation speeds of the Sun over a 12-month period. Red areas represent the fastest rotation, blue the slowest. The cutaway section represents rotation at the Sun's core. **SOHO (ESA & NASA)**

STUDYING THE SUN

The scientific study of the Sun began with the invention of the telescope in the early 17th century. A major breakthrough in solar studies came in the 19th century with the use of spectroscopy—the analysis of the light emitted by the Sun. This approach allowed scientists to determine the composition of the Sun's atmosphere. Scientists in the relatively new field called helioseismology study the Sun's interior by examining waves that travel through it.

USING THE SUN'S SPECTRUM

When a ray of sunlight, which appears white, is passed through a prism or a diffraction grating, it spreads out into a series of colors called a spectrum. Scientists analyze this spectrum to determine what chemicals make up the Sun as well as their abundance, location, and physical states.

In 1814 Joseph von Fraunhofer began a thorough study of the Sun's spectrum. He found that it was crossed by many dark lines, which are now called absorption lines or Fraunhofer lines. Meanwhile, other scientists had been studying the light emitted and absorbed by elements in the gaseous state

when they were heated in the laboratory. They discovered that each element always produced a set of bright emission lines associated with that element alone.

Scientists now believe that the dark lines in the Sun's spectrum represent elements in the Sun's atmosphere. The line that Fraunhofer had called D, for example, was shown to have the same position in the spectrum as the brilliant line that sodium gives off when it is heated in the laboratory. The lines are dark because the elements in the Sun's atmosphere absorb the bright lines given off by the same element on the Sun's disk. Studying the lines of the Sun's spectrum, then, provides a way to study the composition of the Sun's atmosphere. Almost all the elements known on Earth have been shown to exist on the Sun.

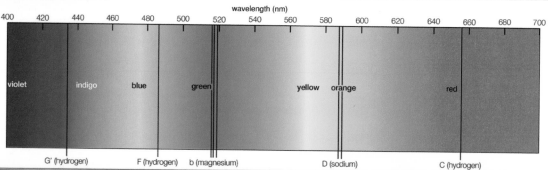

The visible solar spectrum, with prominent Fraunhofer lines representing wavelengths at which light is absorbed by elements. **Encyclopædia Britannica, Inc.**

TELESCOPES AND OTHER INSTRUMENTS

The telescope has been used in solar studies since 1610. The tower solar telescope was later invented for use in solar studies. Its long focal length can give very large images of the Sun. The coronagraph, another special telescope, is used to examine the Sun's outer atmosphere. The instrument blocks the direct light from the Sun's disk, allowing the much dimmer corona to be viewed.

Different layers and features of the Sun's atmosphere emit radiation more strongly at different wavelengths. Solar scientists use instruments that detect radiation at specific wavelengths to study the different parts. For example, the spectroheliograph and the birefringent filter can limit the light that passes through them to a very small range of wavelengths, such as the red light emitted by hydrogen (known as hydrogen alpha) or the violet light of calcium. The photosphere can be seen well in visible light. The chromosphere and the prominences in the corona emit much of their radiation in hydrogen alpha. X rays and extreme ultraviolet are often used to study the corona and solar flares, which emit much radiation at those wavelengths.

On the ground, the effectiveness of a telescope is limited because Earth's atmosphere absorbs much of the Sun's radiation at certain wavelengths. Many orbiting solar observatories and other spacecraft have been launched above the terrestrial atmosphere to study the Sun. Special instruments aboard the craft are used to photograph and measure a variety of solar properties and features, including the Sun's magnetic field and the charged particles of the solar wind.

ANALYZING SOLAR WAVES

Since the Sun's interior cannot be directly seen, solar scientists infer its properties from the behavior of the atmosphere. One method involves studying the oscillations, or pulses, of solar waves. Millions of sound waves and other kinds of waves moving inside the Sun constantly cause some parts of the Sun to move outward and some parts to move inward. In the field of helioseismology, scientists detect and analyze the properties of

A scientist assembles the optical system of a magnetographic telescope, designed to measure magnetic fields that occur between the Sun's photosphere and corona. **NASA**

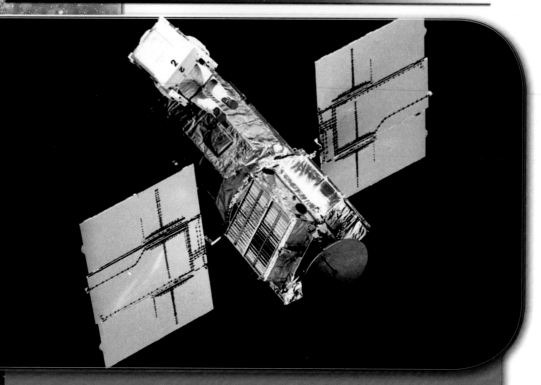

Solar Maximum Mission (SMM) satellite observatory, photographed above Earth during a U.S. space shuttle mission in 1984 to conduct in-orbit repairs of the satellite. Launched in 1980 near the most active part of the solar cycle, the SMM observatory carried several instruments to study solar flares and the solar atmosphere across a range of wavelengths from visible light to gamma rays. An astronaut wearing a space suit with a maneuvering backpack is visible in the upper left of the image. **NASA**

these waves, including the patterns of their oscillations.

In general, the waves travel in one direction until abrupt changes in density or temperature within the Sun's layers

Observing the Sun

Because solar energy is so intense, there are some real dangers in staring at the Sun. Radiation from the Sun's rays can damage one's eyes, so one should never look directly at the Sun with unaided eyes or with a telescope (unless it is equipped with a special solar filter). Dark glasses and smoked glass provide no protection. One safe way to observe the Sun is to project its image through a pinhole or telescope onto a white screen or white cardboard.

bend them back in the opposite direction. Helioseismologists use this information to develop models of the structure and motions of the solar interior. This is similar to the way geologists study the seismic waves produced by earthquakes in order to map Earth's interior.

STRUCTURE AND ENERGY PRODUCTION OF THE SUN

The Sun can be divided into several different layers. Energy is produced in the dense, hot central region, which is called the core, and travels outward through the rest of the interior. The surface, or the part of the Sun that is visible from Earth in ordinary light, is called the photosphere. It emits most of the light and heat that reach Earth.

The surface is the innermost part of the solar atmosphere. The atmosphere also has a thin middle layer, called the chromosphere, and a large outer layer, the corona. The corona gives rise to a flow of charged particles called the solar wind that stretches beyond Earth and the other planets.

ENERGY AND BALANCE OF FORCES

The Sun looks like a burning sphere. It is too hot, however, for an Earth-type chemical reaction such as burning to occur there. Besides, if burning produced its energy, it would have run out of fuel very long ago.

Various theories have been advanced to explain the Sun's tremendous energy output. All the bits of matter in the Sun exert gravitational attraction on each other. One 19th-century theory said that this gravitational attraction causes the Sun to shrink and its matter to become more tightly packed. This process, called gravitational contraction, could release a great deal of energy. However, gravitational contraction would produce energy for only 50 million years at most, while the Sun's age must be at least as great as Earth's age of 4.6 billion years.

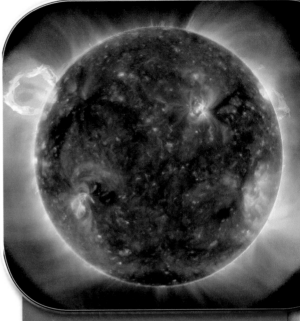

A full-disk multiwavelength extreme ultraviolet image of the Sun, taken by the Solar Dynamics Observatory on March 30, 2010. False colors trace different gas temperatures. Reds are about 60,000 K; blues and greens are greater than 1,000,000 K. NASA/ GSFC/SDO/AIA

In the 20th century, atomic theory finally provided an explanation. Scientists now agree that thermonuclear reactions are the source of solar energy. Albert Einstein's theoretical calculations showed that a small amount of mass could be converted to a great amount of energy. Reactions in the Sun's core convert almost 5 million tons of matter into enormous amounts of energy—3.86×10^{33} ergs—every second. The vast amount of matter in the Sun can provide the "fuel" for billions of years of atomic reactions. Astronomers believe that the Sun is nearly halfway through its "lifetime" of 10 billion years.

The Sun's thermonuclear reactions also keep the star from squeezing inward. While the Sun's gravity exerts a huge inward pull, the energy it produces exerts a huge outward pressure. At this stage in the Sun's life, these forces balance each other out, so that the Sun neither collapses under its own weight nor expands.

CORE

The Sun's core is an extremely hot, dense mass of atomic nuclei and electrons. Its temperature is about 15,000,000 K (27,000,000° F), and it is thought to be some 150 times as dense as water. The pressure is enormous. Normally, protons in atomic nuclei repel each other because they have the same electrical charge. Under the great density and pressure in the Sun's core, however, nuclei can collide and fuse into new and heavier nuclei. This is a type of thermonuclear reaction called a fusion reaction.

The basic fusion process in the Sun involves a series of reactions in which four hydrogen nuclei are ultimately converted into one helium nucleus. The mass of the helium nucleus is about 0.7 percent less than that of the four hydrogen nuclei. This 0.7 percent of the mass is changed into energy. Every second the Sun converts almost 700 million tons of hydrogen into about 695 million tons of helium. Nearly 5 million tons of mass — 0.7 percent of 700 million tons — are converted to energy. Some of this energy heats the plasma in the core and some escapes into space as nearly massless, electrically neutral particles called neutrinos. Some of the energy is in the form of gamma-ray photons. These photons travel outward from the core through a zone in which the energy is carried mainly by radiation. Ultimately, the energy is emitted at the surface in many different wavelengths.

RADIATION AND CONVECTION ZONES

The radiation (or radiative) zone is very dense and opaque. Photons take a long, randomly zigzagged path through it. It takes the energy hundreds of thousands of years, or by some estimates millions of years, to pass through this zone. Gamma-ray photons can travel only a tiny distance before colliding with other particles and being scattered. Farther outward, the photons collide with atoms, which absorb the energy and then reradiate it. The atoms reradiate the energy at progressively longer wavelengths and lower energies. By the time the energy leaves the Sun, much of it is in the form of visible light and infrared radiation (heat).

Surrounding the radiation zone is a cooler region called the convection zone. It takes up about the outer 30 percent of the Sun's interior. In this zone great currents of hot gases bubble upward, while cooler, denser matter sinks (like the circulation in a pot of oatmeal or water boiling on the stove). These currents, called convection currents, transport energy to the surface of the Sun, the photosphere.

PHOTOSPHERE

The photosphere (meaning "sphere of light") is the lowest layer of the Sun visible from Earth. This thin layer is the lowest level in the Sun's atmosphere. Energy finally escapes the Sun from the photosphere, so it is significantly cooler than the solar interior. The temperature at the visible surface is about

5,800 K (10,000° F). The solar atmosphere is also dramatically less dense than the interior.

The photosphere has a definite texture. It is covered with granules, or luminous grainlike areas separated by dark areas. Granules are continually forming and disappearing. Their grainlike structure results from the convection currents that bring hot gases up to the photosphere. Each granule is a convection cell that measures several hundred miles across. The hot upwelling matter appears bright, while the cooler sinking matter appears dark. Periodically, larger darker blotches called sunspots appear on the photosphere. (Sunspots are discussed in Chapter 3.)

The entire surface of the Sun continually vibrates, like the surface of a ringing bell. This up-and-down movement results from the motions of solar waves, which travel inward and outward through the Sun's interior.

CHROMOSPHERE

The layer of the atmosphere above the photosphere is called the chromosphere (meaning "sphere of color"). It is visible as a thin reddish ring around the edge of the Sun during total solar eclipses, when the much brighter photosphere is blocked from view. It can also be

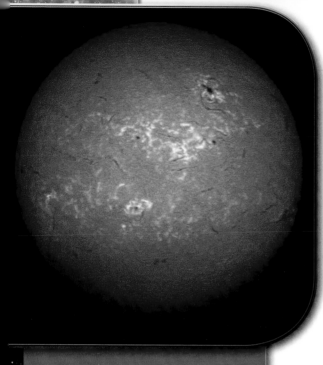

The chromosphere of the Sun observed through a telescope with a filter that isolates the H-alpha emission. Marshall Space Flight Center/National Aeronautics and Space Administration

observed with telescopes with a certain type of filter (hydrogen alpha).

The chromosphere is hotter than the photosphere, and its temperature generally rises with altitude. It is marked by countless jets or small spikes of matter called spicules that continually form and disappear, rising up and falling back down within minutes. Much of the Sun's "weather" takes place in the chromosphere. This includes the violent eruptions called solar flares, which are discussed in Chapter 3.

CORONA

The chromosphere is surrounded by a faintly luminous, extremely thin outer atmosphere called the corona (meaning "crown"). As the corona is a million times dimmer than the Sun's disk, it is usually invisible. It can be seen only when the light of the photosphere

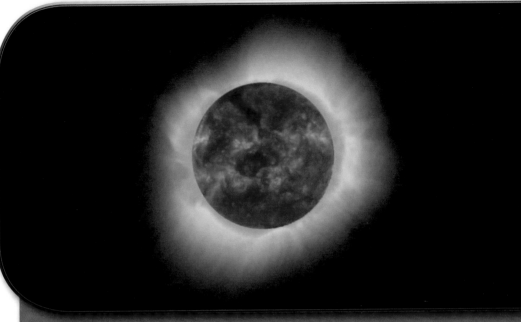

An ultraviolet image of the Moon as it passes in front of the Sun during a solar eclipse. The Sun's corona is clearly visible as a ring of light surrounding the false-color Moon. **NASA/ESA**

is blocked, as in a total solar eclipse or with a special type of telescope called a coronagraph. The corona then appears as a silvery halo with long arcs and streamers.

Much or all of the corona's volume consists of loops and arcs of hot plasma. Counterintuitively, the corona is much hotter than the surface of the Sun. Solar scientists think that energy from the solar magnetic fields heats the corona, but the mechanism for this is not completely clear.

SOLAR ECLIPSES

A solar eclipse occurs when the Moon, revolving in its orbit around Earth, moves across the disk of the Sun so that the Moon's shadow sweeps

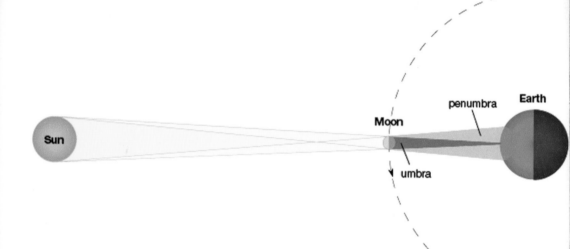

penumbra

Earth

Moon

umbra

Sun

© 2010 Encyclopædia Britannica, Inc.

During an eclipse of the Sun, the shadow of the Moon sweeps over the surface of Earth. In the darkly shaded region (umbra) the eclipse is total; in the lightly shaded region (penumbra) the eclipse is partial. The shaded region on the opposite side of Earth indicates the darkness of night. (The dimensions of bodies and distances are not drawn to scale.) Copyright Encyclopædia Britannica, Inc.; rendering for this edition by Rosen Educational Services

over the face of Earth. No sunlight penetrates the inner part of the shadow, or umbra. To observers on Earth within the umbra, the disk of the Sun appears completely covered by that of the Moon. Such a solar eclipse is said to be total. Because the umbra is narrow at its intersection with Earth, a total eclipse can be observed only within a very narrow area called the zone of totality. Because of the relative motion of Earth and the Moon, the shadow moves rapidly over Earth's surface. A total solar eclipse thus lasts only a short time— less than eight minutes at any one place on Earth. To observers located within the outer part of the Moon's shadow, or penumbra, the disk of the Moon appears to overlap the Sun's disk in part. This event is called a partial solar eclipse.

Because Earth revolves around the Sun in an elliptical orbit, the distance between Earth and the Sun changes slightly during the course of a year. Similarly, the apparent size of the lunar disk changes to some degree during a month because of the elliptical shape of the Moon's orbit. If a solar eclipse occurs when the Sun is closest to Earth and the Moon is farthest away, the Moon does not completely cover the Sun; the rim of the Sun is visible around the edge, or limb, of the Moon. This type of solar eclipse is known as an annular eclipse.

Eclipses of the Sun occur two to four times a year. In rare instances more may occur, as in 1935, when five solar eclipses took place.

The corona is typically about 2,000,000 K (3,600,000° F) at its inner levels. However, this temperature is a measure of the energy of the individual particles in the plasma. The corona's density is so low—the particles of matter are spread out so widely—that the corona does not actually produce much heat. A meteor traveling through the corona does not burn up, as commonly happens in Earth's much cooler but much denser atmosphere.

Although the corona is relatively faint in visible light, it strongly emits radiation at extreme ultraviolet and X-ray wavelengths. However, areas of the corona periodically appear dark at those wavelengths. The corona is extremely thin in these dark areas, called coronal holes. The magnetic fields of the coronal holes open freely into space, and charged particles stream out along the magnetic lines of force. (Magnetic lines of force, or magnetic field lines, show the direction and strength of a magnetic field. Charged particles can easily move through space along these lines but not across them.)

SOLAR WIND

Spacecraft in interplanetary space have encountered streams of highly energetic charged particles originating from the Sun. These streams, called the solar wind, flow radially outward from the Sun's corona through the solar system and extend beyond the orbits of the planets. These particles are continuously released, but their numbers increase greatly following solar flares and other eruptions.

The solar wind is a plasma consisting chiefly of a mixture of protons and electrons plus the nuclei of some heavier elements in smaller numbers. The solar wind may be formed when the hot coronal plasma expands. The particles are accelerated by the corona's high temperatures to speeds great enough to allow them to escape from the Sun's gravitational field.

The fastest streams of the solar wind come from particles that flow from the coronal holes. These particles travel as fast as about 500 miles (800 kilometers) per second. Other streams of the solar wind reach speeds as high as about 250 miles (400 kilometers) per second. These streams usually originate in regions near the solar equator.

As they flow outward, the particles of the solar wind carry part of the Sun's magnetic field along with them. Because of the Sun's rotation and the steady outflow of particles,

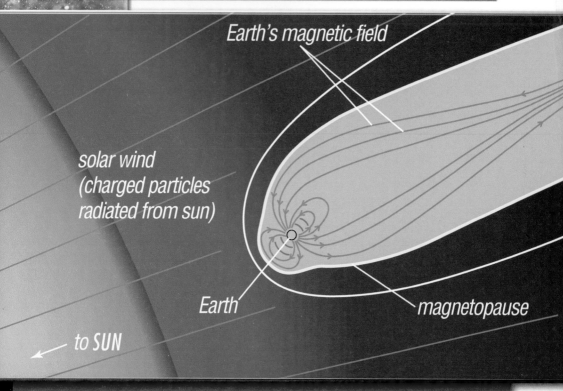

Earth's magnetic field

solar wind
(charged particles
radiated from sun)

Earth

magnetopause

to SUN

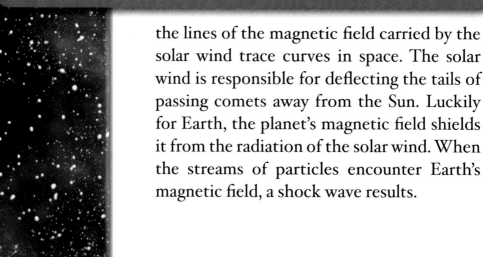

The interaction of the solar wind with Earth's magnetic field causes charged particles to flow around Earth and away from the Sun. Earth's magnetosphere. The magnetosphere's tail is created by the solar wind. Encyclopædia Britannica, Inc.

the lines of the magnetic field carried by the solar wind trace curves in space. The solar wind is responsible for deflecting the tails of passing comets away from the Sun. Luckily for Earth, the planet's magnetic field shields it from the radiation of the solar wind. When the streams of particles encounter Earth's magnetic field, a shock wave results.

THE SUN'S MAGNETIC FIELDS AND SOLAR ACTIVITY

The Sun's magnetic activity is quite complex. Rapid, large fluctuations occur in numerous strong local magnetic fields that are threaded through the Sun's atmosphere. Magnetic activity shapes the atmosphere and causes disturbances there called solar activity. This activity includes sunspots and violent eruptions. Overall, solar activity follows about an 11-year cycle, in which the numbers of sunspots and other disturbances increase to a maximum and then decrease again. The Sun seems to have a weak global magnetic field. Once each 11-year cycle, the north and south poles of the field switch polarity.

SUNSPOTS

Periodically, darker cooler blotches called sunspots temporarily appear on the Sun's surface. Sunspots are areas where very strong local magnetic fields interfere with the normal convection activity that brings heat to the surface. The spots usually appear in pairs or groups of pairs. Each spot typically has a

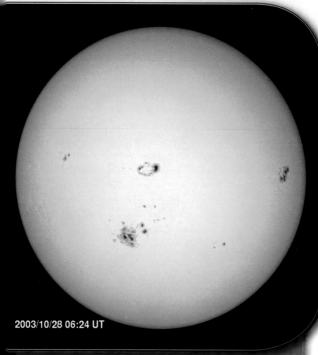

2003/10/28 06:24 UT

Photosphere of the Sun with sunspots, image taken by the Solar and Heliospheric Observatory (SOHO) satellite on Oct. 29, 2003. **SOHO/NASA**

dark, circular center, called the umbra, surrounded by a lighter area, the penumbra. The umbras are about 2,000 K (3,100° F) cooler than the photosphere around them (which means that they are still very hot). Sunspots vary greatly in size but are always small compared to the size of the Sun. When they appear in groups, they may extend over tens of thousands of miles. They last from tens of minutes to a few days or even months.

Regular observations of sunspots have been made since 1750. They reveal that the spots appear and disappear in a cycle and that they are limited to the two zones of the Sun contained between about latitudes 40° and 5° of its northern and southern hemispheres. As mentioned above, the cycle lasts an average of about 11 years. At the beginning of a cycle a few spots appear at around 35° latitudes.

Then they rapidly increase in number, reaching a maximum in the course of around five years. At the same time, the spots get closer and closer to the equator. During the next six years their number decreases while they continue to approach the equator. The cycle then ends, and another cycle starts.

In the early 20th century George E. Hale observed that certain photographs of sunspots showed structures that seemed to follow magnetic lines of force. Often a pair of sunspots appeared to form the north and south poles of a magnetic field. Hale was finally able to establish that sunspots are indeed seats of magnetic fields. In addition, from one 11-year cycle to the next, a total reversal of the sunspots' polarity occurs in the two solar hemispheres. In other words, the north pole of a magnetic field associated with a sunspot pair becomes the south pole, and vice versa. A magnetic cycle of sunspots lasts an average of 22 years, since it encompasses two approximately 11-year cycles.

FLARES

A more violent phenomenon is the solar flare, a sudden eruption in the chromosphere above or near sunspot regions. Flares release

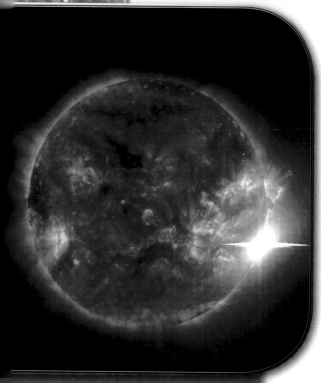

One of the strongest solar flares ever detected appears at right in an extreme ultraviolet (false-color) image of the Sun taken by the Solar and Heliospheric Observatory (SOHO) orbiting spacecraft. Such powerful flares, called X-class flares, release intense radiation that can temporarily cause blackouts in radio communications all over Earth. The flare occurred on Nov. 4, 2003. **SOHO/ESA/NASA**

magnetic energy that builds up along the boundaries between negative and positive magnetic fields that become twisted. The flares usually form very rapidly, reaching their maximum brilliance within minutes and then slowly dying out. They emit huge amounts of radiation at many different wavelengths, including X rays and gamma rays, as well as highly energetic charged particles.

PROMINENCES

Features called prominences also form along sharp transitions between positive and negative magnetic fields. Early astronomers noticed huge red loops and streamers around the black disk of solar eclipses.

An image taken in extreme ultraviolet light reveals a solar prominence lifting off the Sun. The false-color image was captured by the Transition Region and Coronal Explorer (TRACE) orbiting satellite. **TRACE/NASA**

These prominences are areas of relatively cooler, denser plasma suspended like clouds through the hot, low-density corona. Magnetic lines of force hold the plasma in place. Prominences appear as bright regions when seen extending from the solar disk but as long, dark, threadlike areas when seen against the disk. The dark areas are also called filaments.

Long-lived, or quiescent, prominences may keep their shape for months. They form at the boundaries between large-scale magnetic fields. Prominences in active regions associated with sunspots are short-lived, lasting only several minutes to a few hours. When prominences become unstable, they may erupt upward. These eruptions are significantly cooler and less violent than solar flares.

CORONAL MASS EJECTIONS

A type of violent eruption called coronal mass ejections also occurs in the corona. The corona sometimes releases enormous clouds of hot plasma into space. Like solar flares, these coronal mass ejections release energy built up in solar magnetic fields. They usually last hours, however, while the rapid eruptions from flares typically last only minutes.

Like other kinds of solar activity, coronal mass ejections are most common during

A very large coronal mass ejection, at upper right. The red disk in the center is part of the coronagraph used to take the image. The white circle indicates the size and position of the Sun's disk. The false-color image was taken by the Solar and Heliospheric Observatory (SOHO) orbiting space-craft. SOHO/ESA/NASA

GEOMAGNETIC STORMS

The Sun's violent eruptions have concrete effects on Earth. Large solar flares and coronal mass ejections shower Earth with streams of high-energy particles that can cause geomagnetic storms. These storms can disrupt communications satellites and radio transmissions and cause surges in power transmission lines. They also create auroras (the northern and southern lights) near the poles.

Auroras are displays of colored light in the night sky, usually white with a greenish tinge. They may also take on a reddish or yellowish cast. Auroras appear when highly charged particles from sunspots and solar flares excite the thin gases of the upper atmosphere and make them glow. Displays are most frequent in spring and fall because Earth is then most nearly in line with zones of the Sun where sunspots are large and frequent. However, auroras may be most frequent during winter in certain areas.

the solar maximum. Scientists believe that flares, prominence eruptions, and coronal mass ejections are related phenomena. Their relationship is complex, however, and not yet fully understood.

THE STARS:
THEIR PLACE IN THE SKY

S ince ancient times people have gazed at thousands of stars in the night sky. For most of this time, they could only guess about the nature of these pinpoints of light, often making them objects of wonder, worship, comfort, or fear. In the last century, scientists determined what stars are — enormous balls of incandescent gas, powered by nuclear fusion reactions in their cores — and that the Sun is one of them.

ANCIENT IDEAS ABOUT STARS

Many ancient cultures believed that the stars were lights attached to a huge dome (the sky) over Earth. The stars maintained fixed positions relative to each other as they moved nightly across the heavens, as if the sky dome were rotating around Earth.

Ancient people imagined patterns in the stars and grouped them into constellations representing various animals, people, mythological heroes, and even everyday objects. Some cultures attributed godlike powers to the stars and worshipped them. Many also

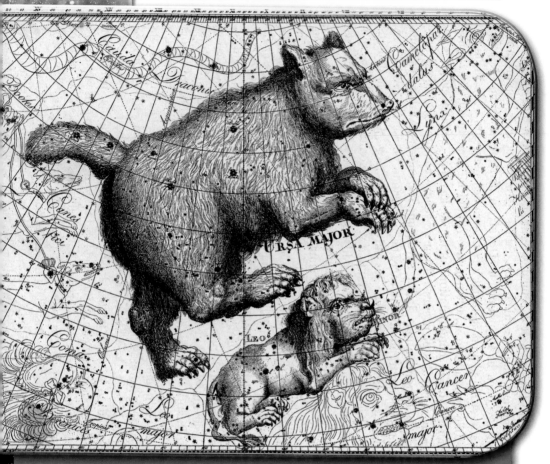

Ancient civilizations ascribed animal and other familiar shapes to patterns of stars, thereby creating constellations such as Ursa Major (top) and Leo Minor (bottom). **Archive Photos/Getty Images**

thought that the motions of the heavenly bodies, particularly of the planets, corresponded to or foretold events on Earth. This belief, shared by many cultures, became the basis of astrology.

CONSTELLATIONS

Many of the constellations have names that are very old. The Sumerian shepherds and farmers of Mesopotamia 7,000 years ago may have called the Bull, the Ram, the Lion, and many other constellations by the same names we use. Students of history are sure these names started in Mesopotamia because the choice of animals suggests this. If the names had first been used in Egypt, there should be a hippopotamus or elephant among the stars. If they had started in ancient India, there should be a tiger or crocodile.

The later people of Mesopotamia took over the old Sumerian names for the constellations and still later the Greeks adopted them. The Greeks added many names of heroes and demigods to the list of constellations. The Romans used the Greek list but translated the names into Latin.

In about AD 150 the Alexandrian astronomer Ptolemy listed the 48 constellations known to him in his book the *Almagest*. In later centuries astronomers added constellations to Ptolemy's list. Some of these later constellations are named for scientific instruments, such as the Sextant, the Compasses, and the Microscope. Others bear the names of birds and beasts in tropical regions (the Giraffe, the Chameleon, the Toucan). Today 88 constellations are recognized by astronomers.

The path of the sun among the stars is called the ecliptic. The 12 constellations that lie along the ecliptic form the zodiac, or birth-sign constellations. The other constellations are divided into those north of the zodiac and those south of it.

More practically, the motions of the stars and planets during the year became the basis for calendars, which were crucial in the development of agriculture. Also, the stars became valuable tools for navigation, especially for seafaring peoples such as the Phoenicians and Pacific Islanders.

MODERN ASTRONOMY

While roots can be traced back through Arab and Greek contributions, modern astronomy started with the work of Nicolaus Copernicus in Poland in the early 16th century. Copernicus concluded that the Sun, not Earth, was the center of the universe and that Earth was a planet orbiting the Sun. This presented problems, though. One such problem was that if Earth moved, the stars—presumed to be on a large, fixed sphere—should appear to observers on Earth to shift back and forth as Earth orbits the Sun once a year. No such shift, called parallax, was seen. This meant that either Copernicus was wrong or that the stars were so distant (at least hundreds of times more distant than Saturn) that the shift could not be detected. The latter turned out to be the case.

The implication that the stars were so far away led some, such as the Italian scholar Giordano Bruno, to suggest that stars were in fact like the Sun, but so distant that they looked dim. He believed that the stars could even have their own planets. Rather than being on a sphere, they were scattered through infinite space. For this and (mainly) for various theological reasons, the Roman Catholic Church burned Bruno at the stake in 1600.

In 1572 the Danish astronomer Tycho Brahe saw a new star appear in the heavens, only to have it fade away within weeks. Ancient authorities had claimed that the stars were eternal and unchanging. Starting in 1609 Galileo Galilei made observations of the heavens with telescopes. His discoveries generally supported the Copernican theory. Additionally, his telescopes revealed great numbers of stars invisible to the unaided eye. This undermined a popular belief that stars were created solely for the benefit of humans.

After this, scientists began to think of stars as natural, physical objects, rather than as gods, mystical beings, or portents. Isaac Newton's work in physics in the late 17th century, combined with advances in instrumentation and the study of light, paved the way for great advances in the understanding of stars.

THE NUMBER AND DISTRIBUTION OF STARS

On a clear dark night, far from the artificial lights of a city, one can see as many as 3,000 stars with the unaided eye at a given time. Waiting through the night, as stars rise and set, or through the year, as different stars are visible in different seasons, extends the number of naked-eye stars to about 6,000.

Two of Galileo's telescopes are displayed at a gallery in Florence, Italy, that was erected in the ancient astronomer's honor. **Hulton Archive/ Getty Images**

Telescopes reveal millions of stars otherwise too dim to be seen. A hazy band of light—the Milky Way—can often be seen stretching across the sky from dark sites away from city lights. Telescopes show this band to be the combined light of hundreds of millions of stars. Astronomers have determined that we live in this band of stars, which extends to form a huge disk-shaped object called the Milky Way galaxy. The Sun is but one of more than 100 billion stars in this group. The number of stars in the observable universe (the universe itself perhaps being infinite) is estimated at roughly 10^{22}—about the number of grains of sand on all the beaches of Earth.

MOTIONS OF STARS

Even casual looks at the sky a few hours apart show the stars moving westward during the night. More careful observation shows that they move as if attached to a large sphere surrounding Earth. The sphere's axis of rotation passes through the North and South poles, so that Polaris (the "North Star")—which lies very close to this axis—appears to barely move. This imaginary sphere rotates once every 23 hours and 56 minutes. The 4-minute difference between this rate and the 24-hour day accumulates to 2 hours per month and a whole day in a year. For this reason, the positions of the constellations, as seen at a certain time of night, can be identified with the seasons. For example, Orion culminates (reaches its highest point in the sky) at about midnight in December, but by March it does so

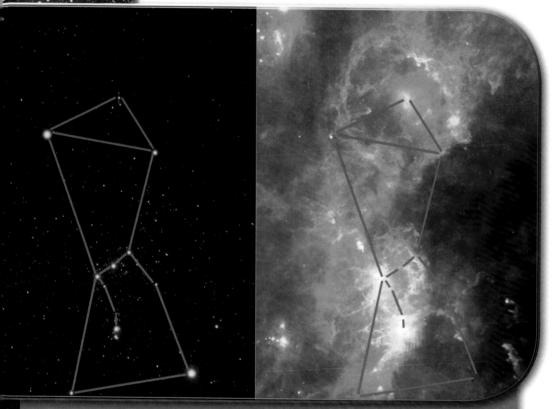

The constellation of Orion in visible (left) and infrared (right) light. The infrared image was taken by the Infrared Astronomical Satellite. Visible light image, left, Akira Fujii; Infrared image, right, Infrared Astronomical Satellite/NASA

at about 6 p.m. In June this happens at about noon, so that it cannot be seen at night. By September it culminates at about 6 a.m. In December it is back where it started.

An observer at the equator eventually gets to see all the stars, by waiting all night or all year. An observer at the North Pole sees only the same stars all the time, and these stars appear to go around in horizontal circles. At the South Pole a completely different set of stars is seen. In the midlatitudes there are some stars that never rise, some that never set, and a large number that rise and set daily. Australians get to see Crux (the Southern Cross) but never the Big Dipper. Observers in the northern United States see the Big Dipper but never the Southern Cross. In both countries Orion appears half the time. These motions are due to Earth's daily rotation on its axis, combined with its yearly revolution around the Sun.

Note that the constellations maintain their shapes as the stars appear to move in lock step. The individual stars actually move independently, however. Their very gradual apparent motions will, after hundreds of thousands of years, make the current constellations unrecognizable. Astronomers call these individual apparent motions "proper motion." A star's proper motion, combined with its motion toward or away from the observer, is used to determine the star's actual velocity, relative to the other stars. This speed can be hundreds of miles per second. The distances to stars are so great, however, that these motions are not noticeable to the naked eye over a human lifetime.

BRIGHTNESS AND DISTANCES OF STARS

Astronomers measure the brightness of stars by means of their magnitude, a concept introduced in ancient times. Apparent magnitude is the brightness of a star as it appears to an observer on Earth. How bright a star looks depends on its distance from the observer, however, so distance must be determined to learn the true brightness of stars. This measure is called absolute magnitude.

MEASURING BRIGHTNESS

Ancient astronomers devised a rating scale for apparent magnitude that is believed to date back to the Greek astronomer Hipparchus in the 2nd century BC. On this simple scale, the brightest stars were ascribed a magnitude of 1, and the dimmest 6. Not all stars given a particular magnitude were of exactly the same brightness, but the scale was useful and has survived (with modifications) to this day.

Modern instruments determine brightness far more precisely. It was found that magnitude 1 stars are roughly 2.5 times as bright as those of magnitude 2, magnitude 2 are about 2.5 times as bright as

The brightest star in the night sky is Sirius, with a magnitude of 1.44. NASA, ESA, H. Bond (STScI), and M. Barstow (University of Leicester)

magnitude 3, and so on. Some stars are dimmer than can be seen with the naked eye and have magnitudes of 7 or more. The faintest stars detected by the largest telescopes are about magnitude 30. Others are brighter than the typical "bright" stars given magnitudes of 1 by Hipparchus, some even having negative magnitudes on this scale. The brightest object in the heavens as seen from Earth—the Sun—earns a magnitude of -26.7.

MEASURING DISTANCE

In Copernicus's time, the annual shift of the apparent positions of the stars could not be seen. Even early telescopes were incapable of detecting it. However, in 1838 Friedrich Wilhelm Bessel used a large telescope to detect the annual parallax of what turned out to be a relatively nearby star: 61 Cygni.

This provided confirmation of Earth's motion around the Sun and also made possible the first calculation of the distance to a star. Using trigonometry and an earlier calculation of the distance to the Sun, Bessel found 61 Cygni to be about 61 trillion miles (98 trillion kilometers) from Earth. A more convenient unit of distance is the parsec, which is the distance of a star showing a parallax of one arc second ($\frac{1}{3,600}$ of a degree) when the observer moves one astronomical unit, which is the average distance from Earth to the Sun—about 93 million miles (150 million kilometers). Another unit is the light-year, or the distance light travels in one year—about 5.88 trillion miles (9.46 trillion kilometers). One parsec equals about 3.26 light-years.

Bessel's distance to 61 Cygni in parsecs was about 3.19, or about 10.4 light-years. (Modern measurements show it slightly farther, at about 11.4 light-years.)

The nearest star to Earth other than the Sun is Proxima Centauri, a dim companion of the brighter pair Alpha Centauri A and B. Proxima Centauri is some 1.29 parsecs (4.2 light-years) from Earth.

ABSOLUTE MAGNITUDE

Once distances to the nearer stars were known, it became possible to compare the actual brightness, called absolute magnitude, of stars. Absolute magnitude is the apparent magnitude a star would have as seen from a distance of 10 parsecs. Using this scheme, the Sun's -26.7 apparent magnitude would diminish by 31.5 magnitudes if it were moved out to 10 parsecs, rendering an absolute magnitude of 4.8. This means that it would be only dimly visible to the unaided eye. On the other hand, the star Deneb, with an apparent magnitude of about 1.3, would appear 8.4 magnitudes brighter, or about -7.1, if it were brought from its actual distance of about 500 parsecs to only 10 parsecs. This means that Deneb is actually 60,000 times brighter than the Sun.

If it were placed where the Sun is, it would vaporize Earth and the other inner planets.

THE HERTZSPRUNG–RUSSELL (H-R) DIAGRAM

A powerful tool for understanding stars is the H-R diagram, devised independently by Ejnar Hertzsprung and Henry Norris Russell in the 1910s. This diagram plots the absolute magnitude of stars on the vertical axis and the spectral type (effectively measuring color or temperature) on the horizontal axis. When a large, random selection of stars is plotted, the majority of the dots form a band from upper left (bright and bluish) to lower right (dim and reddish). This is called the main sequence (though it does not indicate pro-gression in time). The Sun is a main-sequence star, more or less in the middle of the chart. Spica is also a main-sequence star, but on the upper-left end of the band. Main-sequence M stars are so dim that telescopes are required to see even the ones closest to Earth.

The H-R diagram provides astronomers with an additional tool, called spectroscopic parallax, for estimating distances to stars too distant for accurate measurement of par-allax. A star is judged, for example, to be a

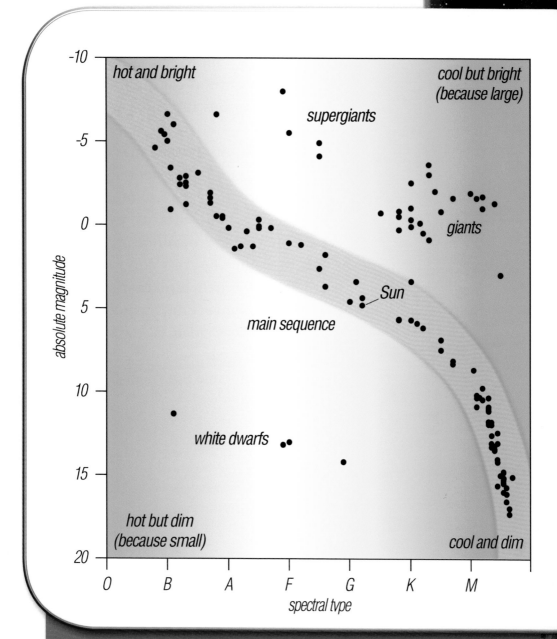

Hertzsprung-Russell diagram. Encyclopædia Britannica, Inc.

main-sequence F7. Comparing its apparent magnitude and estimated (from the diagram) absolute magnitude allows an estimate of its distance. This method can be used even for stars at tremendous distances, in other galaxies.

Not all stars lie on the main sequence. To the upper right are red giants and super-giants. These stars are very bright in spite of having relatively cool surfaces, which do not give off much light per unit area. This means that they must be truly enormous. To the lower left-center are white dwarfs. These stars are quite hot, yet very dim, which means that they must be very small. A few stars are scattered in other areas, such as giant stars above the main sequence but bluer than the red giants.

hapter

THE PROPERTIES OF STARS

To a casual observer on Earth, the stars look like fairly similar points of light. Apart from their locations and differences in apparent brightness, there seems to be little to distinguish one star from the next. In fact, however, stars vary significantly in their physical properties, such as color, temperature, size, and mass. One similarity among stars is their chemical composition—most stars are made up mainly of hydrogen. This gas provides the fuel that stars need to shine.

COLORS, TEMPERATURES, AND COMPOSITIONS

Most people would probably describe stars as "white." However, a careful look shows there are differences. An example is in the familiar constellation Orion, the Hunter. Comparing the star Betelgeuse with the star Rigel shows that Betelgeuse is reddish compared to the slightly bluish Rigel.

In fact, stars generally lie on a spectrum of color from red, through white, to blue. The

Infrared image of the Small Magellanic Cloud, a satellite galaxy of the Milky Way. NASA/JPL-Caltech/STScl

physical reason for this is well understood: bluer stars are hotter. In fact, the surface temperature of a star can be accurately determined from a careful analysis of the color. The visible "surface" of Betelgeuse has a temperature of about 3,500 K (5,800° F), while Rigel is about 11,000 K (19,300° F). The Sun, which appears almost white, is in between, at 5,800 K (10,000° F).

A more careful analysis of a star's light can be made using a spectroscope, which shows just how much light of each wavelength a star gives off. This corresponds to color—blue has a shorter wavelength than red. Dark "absorption lines" in the spectrum indicate certain wavelengths being absorbed by cooler gases in the star's atmosphere, just above the photosphere, or visible "surface." Comparison to the spectra of chemicals on Earth reveals the composition of the star. It turns out that almost all stars consist primarily of hydrogen, along with a lot of helium. A huge variety of other substances, such as oxygen, carbon, silicon, calcium, iron, and even molecules such as titanium oxide, have been found in stellar spectra as well. Stars are so hot that they consist mostly of plasma, or gas whose electrons have been stripped from the nuclei.

Other properties of stars that can be determined using spectroscopes include pressure (which broadens absorption lines), magnetic fields (which split spectral lines in two), and motion toward or away from Earth (which shifts the lines toward the blue or red).

Stars are categorized into spectral types indicated by letters. For historical reasons, the letters are—in order from hottest/bluest to coolest/reddest stars—O, B, A, F, G, K, and M. Numbers 0 through 9 further divide the categories, from hottest to coolest. The Sun, a whitish star, is a type G2.

SIZE

Stars are so distant that even the most powerful telescopes can actually show (resolve) the disks of only some of the larger, closer stars. For most stars, other methods are required to determine size.

A star's position on the H-R diagram gives clues about its size: the upper-right part consists of very large stars, and the lower-left very small. In fact, it is possible to accurately estimate a star's size using the diagram. Some red supergiants are more than 100 times the diameter of the Sun and could easily engulf

Earth's entire orbit around the Sun. White dwarfs are roughly $\frac{1}{100}$ the diameter of the Sun, about the size of Earth itself.

Another way to determine the size of a star is to observe an occultation, which happens when an astronomical object moves in front of another and blocks out its light. An example is when the Moon moves in front of a star. By timing the dimming of the star as the Moon covers it, and knowing the distance to the star, the star's size can be found.

MULTIPLE STAR SYSTEMS

Most stars have companion stars, which they mutually orbit. Often, there are just two, so the system is called a double star or binary star. But other configurations with several individual stars have been found. The multiple nature of some of these star systems is known by direct observation with telescopes. Others are inferred to be multiple through a variety of techniques.

The spectrum of what looks like a single star may show mixed stellar types, indicating that multiple stars are present. Alternating blue and red shifts in the spectrum indicate motion toward and away from Earth. This implies that the star is orbiting an unseen

Two white dwarf stars orbit one another in this artist rendition of an actual binary system known as J0806. NASA/Tod Strohmayer (GSFC)/ Dana Berry (Chandra X-Ray Observatory)

other star (or that a large planet is orbiting it). A wavy path of a star against the background of other stars can indicate the same thing. Periodic dips in the brightness of a star can suggest that another star is passing in front of it and then behind it. Detailed studies of such "eclipsing binaries" can yield information about the sizes, brightness, and shapes of both stars.

EXTRASOLAR PLANETS

Like the Sun, many other stars are accompanied by orbiting planets. These planets, called extrasolar planets, are so distant from Earth, however, that their very faint light is drowned out by the bright light of their "suns." However, the indirect methods used to detect multiple

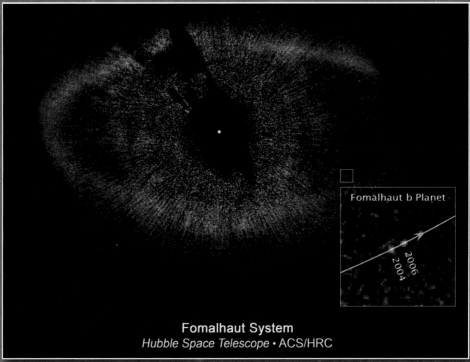

Fomalhaut b Planet

2006
2004

Fomalhaut System
Hubble Space Telescope • ACS/HRC

The extrasolar planet Fomalhaut b in images taken by the Hubble Space Telescope in 2004 and 2006. The black spot at the center of the image is a coronagraph used to block the light from Fomalhaut, which is located at the white dot. The oval ring is Fomalhaut's dust belt, and the lines radiating from the center of the image are scattered starlight. NASA; ESA; P. Kalas; J. Graham, E. Chiang; E. Kite, University of California, Berkeley; M. Clampin, NASA Goddard Space Flight Center; M. Fitzgerald, Lawrence Livermore National Laboratory; and K. Stapelfeldt and J. Krist, NASA/JPL

star systems can also be applied to find extrasolar planets. An orbiting planet causes a star to wobble slightly, and this wobble can be detected as alternating red and blue shifts of the star's light. This technique was first successfully used in 1995 to find a planet orbiting the star 51 Pegasi. It has proven to be the most successful technique by far for finding and studying extrasolar planets. Another detection method measures the dip in light caused when a planet passes in front of a star. By 2010 more than 400 extrasolar planets had been discovered.

MASS AND DENSITY

In a binary star system, the size of the stars' orbits and their orbital periods (the time it takes to complete one orbit) yield very important information. Using these data and Newton's law of gravitation, the masses of both stars can be calculated. Knowing the mass and the size of a star provides the star's density.

HOW STARS SHINE

The first physical explanation offered for the light and heat given off by stars, including the Sun, was that they are simply burning. There are major problems with this explanation, though. First, stars do not contain nearly as much oxygen (needed for burning) as hydrogen. Second, even if they were burning, calculations show that the fuel would be used up quite quickly; the Sun would have burnt out in only a couple thousand years. However, geological evidence and radioactive dating techniques imply that Earth has existed, with the Sun surely shining on it, for more than 4 billion years.

A better explanation was that stars shine by gravitational contraction. Gravity slowly squeezes the stars' gases, thus heating them. This can be a significant source of heat for a star just forming but would supply sufficient energy for only a few tens of millions of years.

The current, almost universally accepted explanation involves the nucleus of the atom and the powerful force that holds it together. The vast majority of the energy produced by stars (at least main-sequence ones) comes from nuclear fusion. Through a series of steps that can vary with the mass of the star, low-mass nuclei (mainly hydrogen) are fused together to make higher-mass (mainly helium) nuclei. This generates roughly a million times the energy of burning and much more than gravitational contraction, thus easily explaining how the Sun could shine so brightly for billions of years. Essentially, stars are slow-burning, gigantic hydrogen bombs.

CHAPTER 5

THE LIVES OF STARS

Using powerful computers, astronomers have been able to simulate the physical conditions in a star throughout its formation and evolution. The following "life story" describes the conditions of a star about the mass of the Sun.

STAR FORMATION AND GROWTH

Before the star is formed, the matter that will one day compose it is found in a large cloud of gas and dust, called a nebula. Such nebulae are abundant in our galaxy. Mutual gravitation among the particles of the nebula causes it to slowly contract. The contraction may be helped along by shock waves from exploding stars or from other external sources of pressure. Gravitational contraction gradually heats the future star until it begins to shine visibly, appearing much like a mature star. The star is "born" when the temperature at the star's core reaches millions of Kelvins—hot enough for the hydrogen nuclei there to move fast enough to collide often enough and hard enough to fuse into helium. The

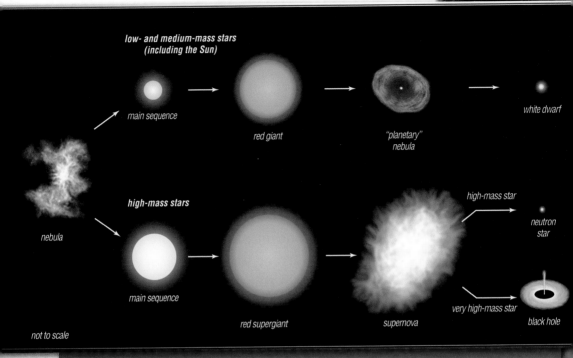

low- and medium-mass stars
(including the Sun)

main sequence

red giant

"planetary" nebula

white dwarf

nebula

high-mass stars

main sequence

red supergiant

supernova

high-mass star

neutron star

very high-mass star

black hole

not to scale

Stellar evolution. **Encyclopædia Britannica, Inc.**

energy released from nuclear fusion produces enough pressure to counteract the inward gravitational pull. The star stabilizes and shines almost steadily for billions of years.

Gradual changes occur, though. As hydrogen in the core is slowly used up and helium "ash" becomes a large fraction of the core's composition, models show that the star grows gradually bigger and brighter. After about 5 billion years from its formation (a point the Sun is approaching), the star is

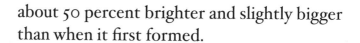

about 50 percent brighter and slightly bigger than when it first formed.

RED GIANTS AND WHITE DWARFS

This process accelerates over the next few billion years. Eventually, all the hydrogen in the core has been used up. Fusion can no longer take place there but instead starts to occur in a layer surrounding the core. The core itself begins to contract under the force of gravity, thus growing hotter. The star begins to expand, ultimately swelling dramatically into a red giant. On the H-R diagram, the star has spent most of its life in the band of the main sequence, but it now rapidly tracks to the upper right.

The red-giant phase is not stable, though, as core temperatures become high enough for fusion of helium into carbon. This sends the star back in the direction of the main sequence on the diagram. After about 100 million years the helium in the core is used up, though, and the contracting carbon core sends the star back into the red-giant state. The star becomes unstable and begins to pulsate. Finally, in one last spasm, the star ejects almost a third of its mass into space, creating an object known as a "planetary" nebula (so-called because of its vaguely similar appearance to the planets Uranus and Neptune as seen through a telescope). As this cocoon of gases dissipates, it reveals the rapidly shrinking core of what had been a gigantic star.

This shrinking core shines brightly, from leftover heat. With fusion energy no longer available, however, gravity compresses the core to about the size of Earth and to a tremendous density—about that of a car smashed down to the size of a sugar cube. Further collapse is prevented by electron degeneracy, an effect of quantum mechanics.

The tiny surface area allows heat to escape so slowly that this corpse of a star—called a white dwarf—shines on for billions of years. It cools so gradually that even the first white dwarfs ever formed in the universe are still glowing about the same color as the Sun.

SUPERNOVAS

Stars starting out with different masses have different fates. Stars about 10 times the Sun's mass pass through the hydrogen-to-helium

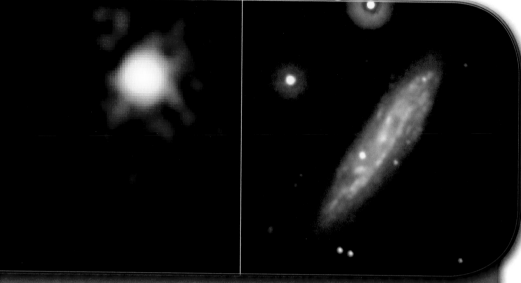

An X-ray image (left) of the exploding star in galaxy NGC 2770 that became Supernova 2008D and a visible-light image (right) of Supernova 2008D captured by the Swift satellite, January 2008. Stefan Immler— NASA/Swift Science Team

fusion process almost 5,000 times faster. These stars swell to red supergiants only a few million years after birth. They then go through multiple pulsations, as they fuse heavier and heavier elements for energy to fight off the crush of gravity. Finally, an ultradense core of almost pure iron, at temperatures of billions of Kelvins, begins to form. After only a day, this core reaches a mass 1.4 times that of the Sun. In a fraction of a second, almost all of the roughly 10^{57} protons and 10^{57} electrons in the core combine to form neutrons, robbing the core of the electron degeneracy pressure that had been preventing its collapse.

The collapse now ensues at a large fraction of the speed of light, crushing the core to a phenomenal density of 10^{14} times that of water—like all the ships in the U.S. Navy crushed to the size of a sugar cube. An effect of quantum mechanics called neutron degeneracy suddenly halts the collapse of the core when it has shrunk to about 10 miles (16 kilometers) in diameter. The core rebounds, however. This sends a titanic shock wave out through the vast surrounding layers of the star, which explode as a supernova.

Such an exploding star releases as much light as billions of main-sequence stars. It shines like this for weeks as the materials spread out into space at tens of thousands of miles per second. The expanding debris can then be incorporated into other nebulae (perhaps also triggering their collapse) and ultimately new stars and planets. In fact, most astronomers think that the elements heavier than helium that make up Earth and its inhabitants were mainly forged in stars and distributed by one or more of such ancient stellar explosions.

PULSARS

In 1967, at the Cavendish Laboratories in Cambridge, England, two astrophysicists happened upon something completely unexpected. Their radio telescope picked up short pulses of energy. At first dismissed as some sort of man-made interference, the pulse was found to recur at regular intervals, much like a "light clock" ticking in space. This was the discovery of the first of a special group of celestial objects called pulsating radio stars, or pulsars for short. These objects emit extremely regular pulses of radio waves, and a few emit short, rhythmic bursts of visible light, X rays, and gamma rays as well. They are thought to be rapidly spinning neutron stars—extremely dense stars composed almost entirely of neutrons and having a diameter of only 6 miles (10 kilometers) or less.

The radiation beams released by a pulsar come from the object's magnetic poles. Because these magnetic poles do not coincide with the pulsar's rotational poles, the rotation of the pulsar swings the radiation beams around. As the beams sweep regularly past Earth with each rotation, an evenly spaced series of pulses is detected by ground-based telescopes. Thus pulsars are not unlike stellar lighthouses.

NEUTRON STARS AND BLACK HOLES

The tiny core of the star remains after the collision. This object, with roughly the mass of the Sun and a diameter of only about 12 miles (20 kilometers), is called a neutron star. Neutron stars generally spin rapidly, and some have strong magnetic fields that focus emitted radiation in beams. If such a beam happens to intercept Earth, observers see the star apparently flashing on and off—sometimes hundreds of times per second. The object is then called a pulsar.

Even more massive stars, with perhaps 30 or more times the mass of the Sun, face an even more extreme fate. After reaching the red supergiant stage and producing an iron core, so much mass—at least 2 or 3 times that of the Sun—remains in the core that nothing can stop the crush of gravity. The collapsing star's gravity becomes so strong that even light cannot escape it, so it is called a black hole.

GALAXIES

S tars are found in huge groups called galaxies. Scientists estimate that the larger galaxies may contain as many as a trillion stars, while the smallest may have fewer than a million. Large galaxies may be 100,000 or more light-years in diameter.

Kinds of Galaxies

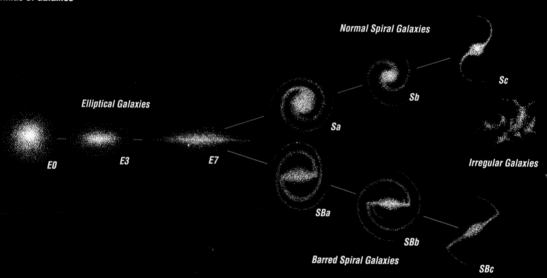

Normal Spiral Galaxies

Sc

Sb

Elliptical Galaxies

Sa

Irregular Galaxies

E0

E3

E7

SBa

SBb

Barred Spiral Galaxies

SBc

In the 1920s Edwin Hubble separated galaxies into four general types according to their appearance—elliptical, spiral, barred spiral, and irregular—and then classified each into subtypes. Encyclopædia Britannica, Inc.

Galaxies may have any of four general shapes. Elliptical galaxies show little or no structure and vary in general shape from moderately flat and round or oval to spherical. Spiral galaxies have a small, bright central region, or nucleus, and arms that come out of the nucleus and wind around, trailing off like a giant pinwheel. In barred spiral galaxies, the arms extend sideways in a short straight line before turning off into the spiral shape. Both kinds of spiral systems are flat. Irregular galaxies are usually rather small and do not have a symmetrical shape.

RADIO GALAXIES

Galaxies were long thought to be more or less passive objects, containing stars and interstellar gas and dust and shining by the radiation that their stars give off. When astronomers became able to make accurate observations of radio frequencies coming from space, they were surprised to find that a number of galaxies emit large amounts of energy in the radio region. Ordinary stars are so hot

The giant galaxy NGC 1316, classified as an ellipitcal galaxy, is also a radio galaxy. **VLT/ESO**

The spiral Whirlpool galaxy (M51), at left, is accompanied by a small, irregular companion galaxy, NGC 5195, at top right. NASA, ESA, S. Beckwith (STScI), and The Hubble Heritage Team (STScI/AURA)

that most of their energy is emitted in visible light, with little energy emitted at radio frequencies. Furthermore, astronomers were able to deduce that this radiation had been given off by charged particles of extremely high energy moving in magnetic fields. These galaxies are called radio galaxies.

ENERGY AND INTERSTELLAR MATTER

Radio galaxies are usually rather peculiar in appearance. Many galaxies, and the radio galaxies in particular, show evidence of interstellar matter expanding away from their centers, as though gigantic explosions had taken place in their nuclei. The giant elliptical galaxy known as M87 has a jet of material nearby that it apparently ejected in the past. The jet itself is the size of an ordinary galaxy.

Astronomers have found that, in many galaxies, stars near the center move very rapidly, apparently orbiting some very massive unseen object. The most likely explanation is that a giant black hole, with millions or even billions of times the Sun's mass, lurks in the center of most large galaxies. As stars and gas spiral into these black holes, much of their mass vanishes from sight. The violent heating and compression produces a huge release of energy, including high-speed jets of matter (such as in M87).

NASA scientists have discovered what they believe to be two mid-size black holes near the center of the starburst galaxy M82 (the Cigar galaxy). The giant black holes at the center of large galaxies may form from the merger of such mid-sized black holes. NASA, ESA, and The Hubble Heritage Team (STScI/AURA)

QUASARS

Very distant galaxies are sometimes found to have extremely energetic sources of light and radio waves at their centers. These objects, called quasars, are generally believed to be several billion light-years from Earth. This means that astronomers who observe quasars are actually peering several billion years into the past. Most astronomers believe that quasars represent an early phase in the life of some galaxies, when the central black holes, with plenty of fresh gas and stars to consume, were generating huge amounts of energy.

DARK MATTER

Another problem has puzzled astronomers for years. Most, if not all, galaxies occur in clusters, presumably held together by the gravity of the cluster members. When the motions of the cluster members are measured, however, it is found in almost every case that the galaxies are moving too fast to be held together only by the gravity of the matter that is visible. Astronomers believe there must be a large amount of unseen matter in these clusters—perhaps 10 times

NGC 1300 is a barred spiral galaxy in the Eridanus cluster. Dark matter accounts for much of the gravitational attraction that holds such galaxy clusters together. NASA, ESA, and The Hubble Heritage Team (STScI/AURA)

as much as can be seen. While some of this likely consists of objects such as black holes and neutron stars, most of it is believed to be dark matter, of unknown origin.

Some dark matter surely consists of well-understood objects such as undetected planets, brown dwarfs (bodies just short of having enough mass to become stars), neutron stars, and black holes. Still, these objects and visible matter together probably make up less than 5 percent of the necessary mass. Computer simulations of early galaxy formation seem to require additional matter, though, to provide enough gravitation to produce the clustering of galaxies seen today. These simulations work well only when this matter is "cold," meaning that its particles are moving slowly relative to each other. This cold dark matter is not made of protons and neutrons like ordinary matter. It is thought to account for another 20–25 percent of the needed mass. All together, these types of matter likely provide about 25–30 percent of the needed mass and therefore seemed to leave the universe open and destined to expand forever.

THE MILKY WAY GALAXY

Like most stars, the Sun belongs to a galaxy. Since the Sun and Earth are embedded in the galaxy, it is difficult for astronomers to obtain an overall view of this galaxy. In fact, what can be seen of its structure is a faint band of stars called the Milky Way (the word *galaxy* comes from the Greek word for "milk"). Because of this, the galaxy has been named the Milky Way galaxy.

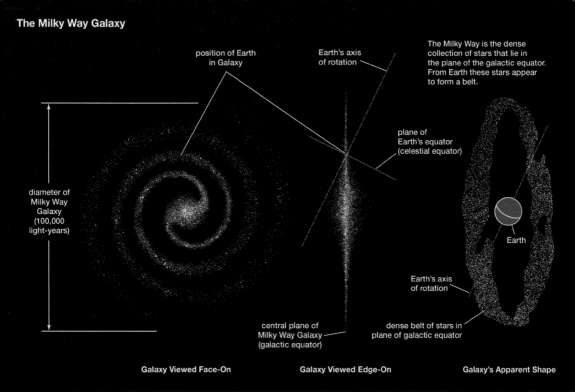

The Milky Way Galaxy

position of Earth in Galaxy

Earth's axis of rotation

The Milky Way is the dense collection of stars that lie in the plane of the galactic equator. From Earth these stars appear to form a belt.

plane of Earth's equator (celestial equator)

diameter of Milky Way Galaxy (100,000 light-years)

Earth

Earth's axis of rotation

central plane of Milky Way Galaxy (galactic equator)

dense belt of stars in plane of galactic equator

Galaxy Viewed Face-On

Galaxy Viewed Edge-On

Galaxy's Apparent Shape

The name of Earth's galaxy comes from the visual phenomenon of the Milky Way, a band of stars seen in Earth's night sky. This band is actually the major portion of the galaxy. Because Earth lies in the midst of the galaxy, the spiral structure is hidden by the nearest stars that lie in the plane of the galactic equator and form the Milky Way. Encyclopædia Britannica, Inc.

SHAPE

The visible band of the Milky Way seems to form a great circle around Earth. This indicates that the galaxy is fairly flat rather than spherical. (If it were spherical, the stars would not be concentrated in a single band.) The Sun is located on the inner edge of a spiral arm. The center, or nucleus, of the galaxy is about 27,000 light-years distant, in the direction of the constellation Sagittarius. All the stars that are visible without a telescope belong to the Milky Way galaxy.

Not all the galaxy's stars are confined to the galactic plane. There are a few stars that occur far above or below the disk. They are usually very old stars, and they form what is called the halo of the galaxy. Evidently the galaxy was originally a roughly spherical mass of gas. Its gravity and rotation caused it to collapse into the disklike shape it has today. The stars that had been formed before the collapse remained in their old positions, but after the collapse further star formation could occur only in the flat disk.

Motions

All the stars in the galaxy move in orbits around its center. The Sun takes about 200 million years to complete an orbit. The orbits of most of these stars are nearly circular and are nearly in the same direction. This gives a sense of rotation to the galaxy as a whole, even as the entire galaxy moves through space.

Nucleus

Dark clouds of dust almost completely obscure astronomers' view of the center of the Milky Way galaxy. Radio waves penetrate the dust, however, so radio telescopes can provide astronomers with a view of the galactic nucleus. In that region stars travel in very fast, tight orbits—which implies the existence of a huge mass at the center. The Earth-orbiting Chandra X-ray Observatory has detected flares of X rays lasting only a few minutes in the region, which are best explained by the existence of a black hole that is violently accelerating and compressing infalling blobs of matter. Infrared observations made at the European Southern Observatory demonstrated that this supermassive black hole has a mass about 4.3 million times that of the Sun.

S tars vary widely in size, mass, brightness, and longevity. The largest are about 100 times the mass of the Sun and about 10 times the Sun's diameter (while on the main sequence, but later swelling by a factor of 100 as red supergiants). They give off almost a million times as much light as the Sun. These large stars burn their fuel so rapidly that they can exist on the main sequence less than $\frac{1}{1,000}$ as long as the Sun. The Sun will remain on the main sequence for an estimated 10 billion years, becoming a white dwarf about a billion years later. The smallest stars, barely able to carry out nuclear fusion in their cores, are roughly $\frac{1}{10}$ the Sun's mass, $\frac{1}{10}$ its diameter, and $\frac{1}{1,000}$ as bright, but they will shine for trillions of years.

The Sun is in some sense an ordinary, mid-size, middle-aged star, but its ranking depends on the group of comparison stars. Compared to the stars one sees in the night sky, it is actually quite small and dim. However, one naturally tends to see only the bigger, brighter stars. Comparing the Sun to all the stars (including the ones too dim to see without a telescope), one finds that it is bigger and brighter than about 95 percent of them.

Considering the Sun in the context of the galaxies provides another point of reference. The Sun is only one member out of more than 100 billion stars in the Milky Way galaxy, and this galaxy is of course not the only such group of stars. Billions of galaxies, some containing up to a trillion stars, are scattered across the observable universe, at distances out to at least 12 billion light-years.

Regardless of how the Sun ranks, however, its relatively steady, bright light, lasting for billions of years, is ideal for life on Earth. Most stars would not make good substitutes.

axis A straight line about which a body or geometric object rotates.

binary star A system of two stars that revolve around each other under their mutual gravitation.

black hole A celestial object that has a gravitational field so strong that light cannot escape it; believed to be created especially in the collapse of a very massive star.

chromosphere The region of the atmosphere of a star, including the Sun, that lies between the star's photosphere and its corona.

corona Outermost region of the Sun's atmosphere, consisting of plasma (hot ionized gas).

galaxy Any of the large groups of stars and associated matter found throughout the universe.

helioseismology A scientific method for studying the Sun's interior by examining waves that travel through it.

parallax The point at which a celestial object, as seen at a distance from two different angles, seems to change direction.

parsec A unit of interstellar measurement equal to about 3.26 light-years.

penumbra The outer part of a cone-shaped shadow cast by a celestial body, where light is partially blocked; compare to umbra.

photosphere The light-emitting surface of the Sun and other stars.

plasma A heated gas consisting of electrically charged particles called ions. Unlike gas, it is a good conductor of electricity.

portent Something that acts as an omen, fortelling events to come.

prominences A solar feature consisting of an area of relatively cooler, denser plasma suspended like a cloud through the hot, low-density corona.

pulsar A celestial object that gives off extremely regular pulses of radio waves and sometimes other forms of radiation. Pulsars are believed to be rapidly spinning neutron stars.

quasar A celestial object at the center of a distant galaxy that emits a great deal of energy.

spectrum A band of color formed when white light is dispersed so that its component wavelengths are arranged in order.

umbra The inner part of a cone-shaped shadow cast by a celestial body, where all light is blocked; compare to penumbra.

American Association of Variable Star
　　Observers (AAVSO)
49 Bay State Road
Cambridge, MA 02138
(617) 354-0484
Web site: http://www.aavso.org
The AAVSO is a nonprofit, scientific and
　　educational organization of amateur and
　　professional astronomers. The organiza-
　　tion collects research on variable stars,
　　or stars that change brightness, from a
　　network of observers located throughout
　　the world.

The Astronomical League
9201 Ward Parkway, Suite 100
Kansas City, MO 64114
(816) 333-7759
Web site: http://www.astroleague.org
The Astronomical League sponsors obser-
　　vation clubs and events and gives awards
　　to amateur astronomers across the
　　United States.

The Astronomical Society of the Pacific
390 Ashton Avenue
San Francisco, CA 94112
(415) 337-1100

Web site: http://www.astrosociety.org

The Astronomical Society of the Pacific
increases the understanding and
appreciation of astronomy through
events, publications, education pro-
grams, and research.

H.R. MacMillan Space Centre
1100 Chestnut Street
Vancouver, BC V6J 3J9
Canada
(604) 738-7827
Web site: http://www.spacecentre.ca

The H.R. MacMillan Centre is a nonprofit
community resource in Vancouver,
Canada. The center inspires interest
in the universe and space exploration
through innovative programming, exhib-
its, and activities.

National Aeronautics and Space
Administration (NASA)
300 E Street SW
Washington, DC 20024
(202) 358-0000
Web site: http://www.nasa.gov

NASA offers information on the U.S. space
program as well as innovative research in

the field of aeronautics. Its site includes games, activities, and other resources for students.

The Royal Astronomical Society of Canada
203-4920 Dundas Street W
Toronto ON M9A 1B7
Canada
(416) 924-7973
Web site: http://www.rasc.ca
Founded in 1868, the Royal Astronomical Society of Canada promotes understanding of astronomy through education, outreach, research, and publications.

WEB SITES

Due to the changing nature of Internet links, Rosen Educational Services has developed an online list of Web sites related to the subject of this book. This site is updated regularly. Please use this link to access the list:

http://www.rosenlinks.com/tss/tssg

Burnell, S. Jocelyn Bell, and others. *An Introduction to the Sun and Stars* (Open Univ.–Cambridge Univ. Press, 2004).

Elkins-Tanton, L.T. *The Sun, Mercury, and Venus* (Chelsea House, 2006).

Golub, Leon, and Pasachoff, J.M. *Nearest Star: The Surprising Science of Our Sun* (Harvard Univ. Press, 2002).

Hubble, E.P. *The Realm of the Nebulae* (Yale Univ. Press, 1982).

Kaler, J.B. *The Cambridge Encyclopedia of Stars* (Cambridge Univ. Press, 2006).

Lang, K.R. *Sun, Earth, and Sky*, 2nd ed. (Springer, 2006).

Miller, Ron. *Stars and Galaxies* (Twenty-First Century Books, 2006).

Morris, Richard. *Cosmic Questions: Galactic Halos, Cold Dark Matter, and the End of Time* (Wiley, 1998).

Pasachoff, J.M. *A Field Guide to the Stars and Planets,* 4th ed. (Houghton, 2000).

Phillips, K.J.H. *Guide to the Sun* (Cambridge Univ. Press, 1995).

Spangenburg, Ray, and Moser, Kit. *The Sun* (Watts, 2001).

Spence, Pam. *Sun Observer's Guide* (Firefly, 2004).

Wilson, D.A. *Star Track: Plotting the Locations of the Stars Within 30 Light-Years of Earth* (Lorien House, 1994).